Tall Tales Theatre Company and **Solstice Arts Centre**
in association with the **Dublin Theatre Festival**
present the premiere of

HALCYON DAYS

by Deirdre Kinahan

HALCYON DAYS was first performed in preview at
Solstice Arts Centre, Co. Meath, on 4 October 2012.
It received its Irish premiere at Smock Alley Theatre as part of the
Dublin Theatre Festival on 10 October 2012.

HALCYON DAYS was originally devised as a short play for the
Abbey Theatre's reading series 'The Fairer Sex' in 2009 and
subsequently developed by Tall Tales Theatre Company with the
support of The Stewart Parker Trust.

Tall Tales Theatre Company would like to give particular thanks to:

The Arts Council of Ireland
Dublin Theatre Festival
Meath County Council
Solstice Arts Centre
The Stewart Parker Trust

HALCYON DAYS

by Deirdre Kinahan

Cast

Anita Reeves
Stephen Brennan

Director	David Horan
Script Mentor	Graham Whybrow
Set & Costume Designer	Maree Kearns
Lighting Designer	Kevin Smith
Sound Designer	Trevor Knight
Choreographer	Muirne Bloomer
Producer	Rob Furey
Stage Manager	Stephanie Ryan
ASM	Tracy Martin
Publicist	Zoetrope
DTF PR	Gerry Lundberg PR
Photography	Patrick Redmond
Marketing	Emma Loughney
Student Intern	Emma Finnegan

Cast and Creative Team

Anita Reeves (PATRICIA WHELAN)

Anita's career has spanned a wide variety of roles. Some of her favourites include: Ruth in *Pirates of Penzance* (Olympia Theatre); Buttercup in *H.M.S Pinafore* (Gaiety Theatre/Old Vic); Ugly Sister in *Cinderella* (Gaiety Theatre Pantomime); *Shirley Valentine* (Tivoli Theatre); Ginnie Gogan in *The Plough and the Stars*, Juno in *Juno and the Paycock* (both at Gaiety Theatre/West End); Mary in *A Life* (Olympia Theatre); Mrs Hardcastle in *She Stoops to Conquer*, Mrs Malaprop in *The Rivals*, Ma in *Da* and the Nurse in *Romeo and Juliet* (Abbey Theatre); Jane in *Absurd Person Singular*, Barbara in *Major Barbara* and Mrs Lovett in *Sweeney Todd* (Gate Theatre); Onoria in *Naked* (Almeida Theatre/Playhouse, London); Shaughraun's mother in *The Shaughraun* (Abbey Theatre/West End). Anita originated the part of Maggie in *Dancing at Lughnasa* for which she was nominated for an Olivier Award (Abbey Theatre/National Theatre/West End) and Kate in the original production of *The Cripple of Inishmaan* (National Theatre). Most recently Anita was nominated for both an Irish Times and Edinburgh Fringe Award for Best Actress as Kay in *Little Gem* (Dublin/Edinburgh/London/Paris/Australia/New York). Her film work includes *Angel, Alarm, Into the West, Butcher Boy* and *Adam and Paul*.

Stephen Brennan (SEAN CEABHRUILL)

Stephen most recently played Lord Illingworth in *A Woman of No Importance* (Gate Theatre). Other recent theatre includes: *My Cousin Rachel, The Speckled People, Hay Fever* (Gate Theatre/2012 Spoleto Festival, Charleston, USA); *Jane Eyre, Death of a Salesman,* Garry Essendine in *Present Laughter* (which also transferred to Spoleto Festival in Charleston); *The Real Thing, Private Lives, Waiting for Godot* (national tour and worldwide); *Old Times, The Pinter Landscape* (Lincoln Centre, New York); Higgins in *Pygmalion*, Rochester in *Jane Eyre*, Mr Darcy in *Pride and Prejudice*, Serge in *Art* and title roles in *Tartuffe* and *Cyrano de Bergerac*. He has also appeared in *Plaza Suite* and *Phaedra* (Rough Magic); *Blackbird* (Landmark Productions); *The Shaughraun* (Albery Theatre, London); *The Life of Galileo* (Project). He appeared in several musicals before becoming a member of the Abbey Theatre for eight years, in 1975, playing a wide variety of roles including in *She Stoops to Conquer, Philadelphia, Here I Come!, A Life, Da*, and was the Abbey's first Hamlet in 1983. His other favourite roles include: Frank-N-Furter in *The Rocky Horror Show*, Petruchio in *The Taming of the Shrew* and Oedipus at the Gaiety. Film and television includes: *The Tudors, Eat the Peach, The General, The Boys from Clare, A Piece of Monologue* and *Waiting for Godot* for Beckett on Film, *Twice Shy, El Cid, Ballykissangel, Father Ted, Bachelor's Walk*.

Deirdre Kinahan (Writer)

Deirdre is currently under commission to Fishamble: The New Play Company, Dublin. She is co-writing her first feature film with the support of the Irish Film Board and working with Altered Image Films in London on her first television drama. She is also under commission to BBC Radio 4 for a new radio play. Deirdre's play *MOMENT* received its US premiere in Chicago in July 2012 and Canadian premiere at La Licorne, Montreal, in October. The Chicago run was extended and moved to a larger theatre due to popularity. She has two other plays in development. Writing for theatre to date includes: *Broken* (Fishamble, 2012); *66 Books* (Bush Theatre, 2011); *Where's My Seat* (Bush Theatre, 2011); *BOGBOY* (Tall Tales & Solstice Arts Centre at Irish Arts Centre/New York/Project Arts Centre); *MOMENT* (Tall Tales & Solstice Arts Centre/Project Arts Centre/Bush Theatre/ national Irish tour); *Salad Day* (Abbey Theatre); *Hue & Cry* (Bewley's Café Theatre & Tall Tales/Glasgow/Romania/Bulgaria/Paris/New York); *Melody* (Tall Tales/Glasgow/national tour); *Attaboy Mr Synge* (Civic Theatre/national tour); *Rum & Raisin* (Tall Tales & Nogin Theatre Co./national tour); *Summer Fruits* (Tall Tales/national tour); *Knocknashee* (Tall Tales & Civic Theatre/national tour); *Passage* (Tall Tales/Civic Theatre); *Bé Carna* (Tall Tales/national tour/ Edinburgh Fringe Festival). For children: *Maisy Daly's Rainbow* (Tall Tales & Solstice); *Rebecca's Robin* (Bewley's Café Theatre); *Show Child* (Livin Dred); *The Tale of the Blue Eyed Cat* (Livin Dred). Radio includes: *BOGBOY*.

David Horan (Director)

David graduated from the Samuel Beckett School of Drama, Trinity College, with a BA in English and Theatre Studies. He is Artistic Director of Bewley's Café Theatre and a freelance theatre director. Directing highlights include: *MOMENT* by Deirdre Kinahan (Bush Theatre, London); *Hue and Cry* by Deirdre Kinahan (Project and Solstice Arts Centre); *Macbeth* and *Dancing at Lughnasa* by Brian Friel (Second Age); *Dear Frankie by Niamh Gleeson* (Gaiety Theatre); *In the Pipeline*, a new play by Gary Owen (Paines Plough/Òran Mór Theatre, Glasgow); *The Death of Harry Leon*, a new play by Conall Quinn (Ouroboros Theatre Company; winner of the Stewart Parker Award for Best New Play 2009); *Danti-Dan* by Gina Moxley and *Way to Heaven* by Juan Mayorga (Galloglass); *Metamorphosis* by Franz Kafka (Once-Off Productions, part of the Rep Experiment); *Wallflowering* by Peta Murray (Tall Tales); *Can You Catch A Mermaid?* and *Peter Pan* (Pavilion Theatre @ Christmas); *The World's Wife, Lady Susan, To Kill A Dead Man*, and the award-winning *Tick my Box!* (all with Inis Theatre). David is also an award-winning screenwriter, having co-written *Belonging to Laura*, a contemporary film adaptation of *Lady Windermere's Fan* (Accomplice/TV3) and *The Importance of Being Whatever*, an adaption of *The Importance of Being Earnest* (IFTA Winner 2012).

Maree Kearns (Set & Costume Designer)

HALCYON DAYS is Maree's second production with Tall Tales, having previously designed *MOMENT* in 2010/11. Most recently she has designed *Macbeth* for Second Age Theatre Company, for whom she has also designed *Dancing at Lughnasa* and *Hamlet*. Other theatre designs include: *The Goddess of Liberty* (Guna Nua Theatre Company); *Plasticine* (Corcadorca Theatre Company); *Happy like a Fool* (Red Kettle Theatre Company); *Ragús – The show* and *Dear Frankie* (Verdant Productions); CoisCeim Dance Theatre's double bill: *As You Are* and *Faun, Splendour* (RAW/Project Arts Centre); *84 Charing Cross Road* and *Over & Out* (Lane Productions). She has worked extensively as the set and costume designer with Livin' Dredd Theatre Company and Nomad Theatre Network, whose productions number amongst them: *Observe the Sons of Ulster Marching Towards the Somme* for which she received the 2009 Irish Times Best Set Design Award, *The Dead School* (Irish Times Best Costume Designer & Best Production Nominee 2008); *Conversations on a Homecoming, There Came a Gypsy Riding, Heading for Dakota* and *Shoot the Crow*. She was the design co-ordinator for the Abbey and Peacock Theatres during their centenary year. Maree has also worked as production designer and in art departments on many Irish and international television series, films, advertising and documentary dramas.

Kevin Smith (Lighting Designer)

Kevin trained at the Samuel Beckett Centre, Trinity College, and holds a BA (Hons) in Drama and Theatre Studies. His theatre design credits include: *Serious Money, Dying City* (Rough Magic); *Heading For Dakota* (Livin Dred); *Buck Jones and the Body Snatchers* (Joan Sheehy Productions); *Excess Baggage, The Fisherman's Son* (Belltable); *84 Charing Cross Road* (Lane Productions); *Fairytale Heart* (Calypso); *Grumpy Old Women* (Gaiety); *Rhinoceros* (Blue Raincoat Theatre Company). Kevin's opera work includes: *Madama Butterfly* (Opera Ireland); *Orpheus in the Underworld* (Gleeson Theatre); *Flatpack* with Ulysses Opera Theatre Company. His dance credits include: *Exodus* and *Grand Junction* (Dance Theatre of Ireland); *Between Earth Sky & Home, Triptik, Frame* (Citóig), *The Ballet Ruse* (Muirne Bloomer & Emma O'Kane) and most recently *Step Up* with John Jaspers and Liz Roche, and *An Outside Understanding* with Croí Glan.

Trevor Knight (Sound Designer)
Trevor was a keyboard player in the 1970s with Irish bands *Naima* and *Metropolis*. In 1980 in Holland, he formed *Auto da Fe* with singer Gay Woods. They recorded three albums – *Tatitum*, *Five Singles and One Smoked Cod*, and *Gazette* – touring Ireland and the UK extensively. He has recorded and performed with artists such as Paul Brady, Philip Lynott, Mary Coughlan, Luka Bloom, Camille O'Sullivan, Roger Doyle and Donovan. He has written more than sixty scores for theatre including *Catalpa* by Donal O'Kelly (Edinburgh Fringe Festival), which won a Fringe First and toured the world, *Juno and the Paycock* (Abbey Theatre), and *Circus* for Barabbas (toured to USA). As theatre director, shows include: *Bleeding Poets*, *The Remarkable Rocket*, *Just a Little One – A Dorothy Parker Cocktail* and *The Whistling Girl*, in which he set poems of Dorothy Parker to music. He composed the music, conceived and directed *slat*, featuring Japanese Butoh dancer Maki Watanabe (Galway Arts Festival/Dublin Theatre Festival/Centre Culturel Irlandais, Paris) and *The Devil's Spine Band* (Galway Arts Festival/Smock Alley Theatre, Dublin). Film soundtracks include: *Double Carpet* (Channel 4) and *What am I Doing Here* (Trish McAdam). He has collaborated many times with artist Alice Maher including: *The Music of Things*, *Godchildren of Enantios* (Dublin, London and New York) and is currently completing sound work on *Cassandra's Necklace* which will be shown in IMMA as part of Alice's upcoming retrospective. He is a member of Aosdana since 2007.

Stephanie Ryan (Stage Manager)
Having started her career in 1993 with The Passion Machine Theatre Company, Stephanie has worked with many companies over the years. These include the Abbey Theatre, Opera Theatre Company, Opera Ireland, Fishamble and CoisCéim to name a few. Her most recent work was with Rough Magic on *Travesties, The House Keeper, Improbable Frequency* and *Plaza Suite.* She has also recently toured extensively with the Abbey Theatre's production of *Terminus* to the USA, UK and Australia. She is delighted to have the opportunity to work with Tall Tales on *HALCYON DAYS.*

TALL TALES THEATRE COMPANY

'Tall Tales Theatre Company offer a fresh and brilliant reminder of different approaches to theatre'
Scotsman on *Melody*

Founded in 1997, Tall Tales Theatre Company commission and produce new Irish theatre, premiere international plays and playwrights, tour productions and provide for professional development and theatre participation in Co. Meath, Ireland.

'Incisive directing...
accomplished actors...
a remarkably vivid debut'
New York Times on *Hue & Cry*
by Deirdre Kinahan

'A great production from
Tall Tales... comic, caustic...
you know you are in safe hands as
soon as you take your seat'
The View (RTÉ) on *Wallflowering*
by Peta Murray

'A seamless production in which all
elements combine cleverly
to create great theatre'
Irish Times on *Rum 'n' Raisin*
by Alice Barry & Deirdre Kinahan

'A beautiful fluid production...
emotionally charged and moving'
Irish Times on *BOGBOY*
by Deirdre Kinahan

Artistic Director: Deirdre Kinahan

Tall Tales Theatre Company, Solstice Arts Centre, Navan, Co. Meath
www.talltales.ie   info@talltales.ie   +353 (0)46 9092310

TALL TALES ARE SUPPORTED BY THE ARTS COUNCIL OF IRELAND
SOLSTICE ARTS CENTRE AND MEATH COUNTY COUNCIL ARTS OFFICE

Solstice Arts Centre

Solstice Arts Centre is a multidisciplinary centre for the arts located in Navan, Co. Meath. Its facilities consist of a tiered 320-seat theatre, visual-arts spaces, studio and café. Since opening in 2006, Solstice has exhibited, curated and commissioned a diverse range of exhibitions, theatre and music events, gaining national and international recognition.

Solstice Arts Centre is committed to presenting and commissioning works of artistic and cultural importance, embracing a vibrant local arts community and connecting strongly with a core, loyal audience.

Tall Tales Theatre Company has been in residency in Solstice Arts Centre since January 2008. During this time Solstice Arts Centre has presented, commissioned and co-produced numerous Tall Tales productions.

Artistic Director: Belinda Quirke

Solstice Arts Centre, Railway Street, Navan, Co. Meath
Telephone: +353 (0)46 909 2300
Email: info@solsticeartscentre.ie   Visit: www.solsticeartscentre.ie

Culturefox.ie

Culturefox.ie is the definitive online guide to Irish cultural events, giving you complete information about cultural activities both here and abroad.

To find out what's on near you right now, visit **Culturefox.ie** on your computer or mobile phone.

Culturefox.

Download the FREE App
available now for:

iPhone | Android | Blackberry

comhairle chontae na mí
meath county council

Meath County Council Arts Service

County Meath lays claim to some of the most significant
cultural and artistic jewels in Ireland's crown. Symbols
associated with The Book of Kells and Newgrange have
come to have national and international currency,
representing the rich heritage of Ireland's past. Meath
County Council is proud to be at the forefront of support for
artists and their work in contemporary Meath, support for
which ensures meaningful arts experiences for the county's
citizens.

Meath County Council Arts Service works closely with artists,
individuals and communities to increase access to,
awareness of and participation in the arts across all
disciplines and sectors of society. It achieves this through
the provision of an annual series of cultural events which
include music, dance, theatre, visual art, literature, and
participatory arts projects. It also provides a wide variety of
funding opportunities for artists and groups of all disciplines,
amateur and professional, and a comprehensive information
and advice service. It also acts as a facilitator for arts
organisations and plays a major role in the development of
good practice for the county. 2006 saw the completion and
opening of the County's first arts centre – the award-winning
Solstice Arts Centre, Navan.

In 2012 five new public art features have been installed
throughout Co. Meath with more still to follow. There will also
be a number of premieres of Meath County Council
commissions across a range of disciplines. These actions
are intended to support the Local Authority policy of
supporting quality artistic endeavour, provision of
employment opportunities for artists and long-term
sustainability and durability for the arts in the county.

Meath County Council is proud to be associated with Tall
Tales Theatre Company and wishes them continued success
with this and future productions.

Dublin Theatre Festival

Dublin Theatre Festival is Europe's oldest specialist theatre festival and has been on the world's festival calendar since 1957. Dublin Theatre Festival runs annually for eighteen days across September and October.

The Festival presents major international theatre of scale, and has hosted productions by the world's most highly regarded artists, while also premiering work of celebrated Irish writers. Within the theatre festival, we present many different programme strands which incorporate everything from music to dance, from cutting-edge theatre to the biggest shows on Broadway! Our mandate is simple. If it's the best in the world, it is coming to the Festival!

Apart from hundreds of main-stage performances, we also present a programme of special events which include masterclasses from the world's leading theatre artists, artist-development programmes, film screenings, talks and critical events.

Dublin Theatre Festival
44 East Essex Street, Temple Bar, Dublin 2
www.dublintheatrefestival.com
00 353 (0)1 677 8899

The Stewart Parker Trust

The Stewart Parker Trust pays tribute to the northern playwright through projects supporting emerging writers for the theatre in Ireland; early in his career, Stewart had difficulty in gaining financial backing or access to theatre managements when trying to have his work read or produced.

Each year, the Trust identifies the writers having their first professional production of a play in Ireland, and makes three awards – a Major Bursary, the BBC Radio Drama Award and the BBC Irish Language Award. And there is the option of a week-long workshop at the Tyrone Guthrie Centre with Graham Whybrow, the former Literary Manager of the Royal Court Theatre in London and a leading international consultant on new playwriting. Also on offer are connections with publishers, agents and foreign festivals and production companies.

Recipients of Trust awards include Sebastian Barry, Conor McPherson, Mark O'Rowe and Enda Walsh, and most of the writers of this generation currently feeding new energy into Irish theatre.

The most recent development in the Trust's activities is the Playwright Mentoring Programme, which allows writers already established in Irish theatre, like Deirdre Kinahan, to spend time in consultation with Graham Whybrow on the development of their new work.

IRISH THEATRE INSTITUTE
creating opportunities abroad strengthening resources at home

Irish Theatre Institute

Irish Theatre Institute is a resource organisation that supports and acknowledges the achievements and ambition of Irish theatre artists and companies across all aspects of theatre practice. ITI's mission is to create opportunities abroad and strengthen resources at home for theatre artists, companies, venues and festivals. ITI has pioneered networking, information provision and on-line research tools and promotes the Irish play repertoire through PLAYOGRAPHYIreland, a searchable catalogue of all new Irish writing in English and Irish since 1901. ITI also runs an artist-development initiative, Six in the Attic, which provides six theatre artists with space and practical resources to develop their work in a mentored environment.

Tall Tales would like to thank

Our Amazing Cast and Crew for *HALCYON DAYS*
Belinda Quirke and all at Solstice Arts Centre
John Fairleigh and the Stewart Parker Trust
Erin Kenny
Willie White and all at Dublin Theatre Festival
Smock Alley Theatre
David Parnell and all at The Irish Arts Council
Gerardette Bailey and Cathy Martin
    and all at Meath County Council Arts Office
Tom Dowling
Nick Hern and all at Nick Hern Books
Lily Williams and all at Curtis Brown
Jane Daly and all at the Irish Theatre Institute
Christine Sisk and all at Culture Ireland
Bob Shaw
Johnny Walsh
Maureen Collender
John Hanley
Ronan Kinahan at Vibe Training
Rena Collender
The Tyrone Guthrie Centre
Bellinter House Hotel
Tracy Martin
Jonathan Arun
Mark O'Halloran
Aideen Howard
Bairbre Ni Caoimh
Rosaleen Linehan
Des Cave
Gary O'Farrell
Susan Connolly
Brid Dukes
Dublin County Council Arts Office
John Kinahan

HALCYON DAYS

Deirdre Kinahan

For Uncle Sean

Characters

SEAN CEABHRUILL, *seventy-two*

PATRICIA WHELAN, *sixty-seven*

Set

We are in the conservatory of a nursing home in Dublin. There
are three areas: The Home, The Conservatory and The Garden.
Most of the action takes place in the conservatory which is
somewhere in-between, a kind of holding area, where everything
is essentialised. When they move into the garden, the sunshine
becomes almost like a third character, everthing shifts. I imagine
something like a bell jar. I have the notion of a shifting set?
Whilst they are static through illness and age, their dynamic is
constantly shifting, unearthing. They are in the same room but
we see it from different perspectives – perhaps it revolves?

D.K.

*This text went to press before the end of rehearsals and so may
differ slightly from the play as performed.*

Scene One

SEAN *is alone in an armchair in the conservatory of a North County Dublin Nursing Home. There is a cake box on the table in front of him – also a lady's handbag and car keys.* PATRICIA *enters from the garden – she struggles with the sliding door.*

PATRICIA. Jesus, but does anything do what it's supposed to do in this place?

There is no response from SEAN.

No doubt this seat will collapse as soon as I sit in it!

Still no response.

She makes a big affair of sitting down. Rocks the chair to be sure it will hold her, etc.

I said it to the matron.

'This place is a disgrace,' I said. 'Falling apart,' I said.

'I can't see where you spend the exhorbitant fees!'

Not a word from her, of course. Just a smile – and that taut it looked like it might crack her face.

Pause. She looks at SEAN.

Hello!

There is no response.

Hello, hello!

Still no response.

Dear God help me…

There is the sound of a tea trolley. SEAN *looks around.*

Well, that got your attention!

He looks at PATRICIA *as if she has just entered – as if he has awoken. He attempts to stand.*

SEAN. Good day.

PATRICIA *looks around. He sits again.*

PATRICIA. Good day yourself.

SEAN. Tea?

PATRICIA. It's not here yet.

SEAN. Would you like some tea?

PATRICIA. No, it's not here yet… she's in the TV room.

SEAN. Ahhhh…

Apologies.

PATRICIA. No problem. She'll surely be here in a minute.

SEAN. Yes.

PATRICIA. Though the tea will no doubt be cold.

SEAN. Yes.

PATRICIA. And stewed!

SEAN. Lovely.

Pause.

PATRICIA. It's quiet in here at any rate.

No response.

I said it's quiet in here!

SEAN. Oh, it is. It is.

PATRICIA. Peaceful.

SEAN. Very peaceful.

Pause.

PATRICIA. Not like that day room.

Her look demands a response.

SEAN.... no

PATRICIA. A zoo!

SEAN. Oh yes.

PATRICIA. Can you believe there's a one in there doing yoga?

SEAN. Yogurt...?

PATRICIA. For the infirm!

Ridiculous.

She claims it's good for the bones.

SEAN. Yogurt?

PATRICIA. She was in an unnatural twist at any rate, when I left... and the sight of the four in train!

I mean, there's few enough can walk in this place, let alone yoga!

You could see it was a struggle for them just to keep the porridge down.

SEAN *laughs*.

PATRICIA *is pleased*.

Slight pause.

I am Patricia Whelan.

Again he tries to stand.

No, no, don't stir yourself.

He puts out his hand.

SEAN. Sean.

PATRICIA. Hello, Sean.

SEAN. Sean Ceabhruill.

PATRICIA. Sean Ceabhruill?

SEAN. Yes.

PATRICIA. I know that name.

SEAN. Do you?

PATRICIA. I know I know that name…

SEAN. Marvellous.

PATRICIA. Are you from Dublin?

SEAN. No.

PATRICIA. Rathfarnham?

SEAN. No.

PATRICIA. Do you have relatives there?

SEAN. No.

PATRICIA. But I know that name?

SEAN. Rathmines…

PATRICIA. You're from Rathmines?

SEAN. No.

PATRICIA. I taught some Flynns from Rathmines.

SEAN. Quinns?

PATRICIA. Do you know the Flynns?

Alicia, Bernard, Florence –

Ludicrous names like that.

SEAN. Flynns?

PATRICIA. Do you know them?

SEAN. Eh… no.

PATRICIA. And there were the Collins twins…

Did you know the Collins twins?

SEAN. I… I'm afraid not.

PATRICIA. And are you sure you're from Rathmines?

SEAN. No… no. Tipperary!

PATRICIA. Tipperary?!

SEAN. Yes.

N… N… Nenagh.

PATRICIA. But I don't know anyone from Nenagh!

SEAN. Oh… I'm sorry.

PATRICIA. You said… RATHMINES.

SEAN. Rathmines.

Stumbling.

Rathmines is my home…

PATRICIA. Oh. I see.

SEAN. Yes.

PATRICIA (*like a teacher*). Very good – very good, Sean.

He smiles, relieved.

Another pause.

And whereabouts in Rathmines?

SEAN. Oh…

PATRICIA. Lenister road?

SEAN. No.

PATRICIA. Grove Park?

SEAN (*rushes in*). 12 Grosvenor Square Dublin 6W.

PATRICIA. Oh! very nice.

And do you rent in Rathmines?

SEAN. No. It's my… it's my… it's my… (*Has lost the word.*)

PATRICIA. Home?

SEAN. Yes.

PATRICIA. Very good.

SEAN. Thank you.

She pauses. She smiles. He smiles.

PATRICIA. So what are you in for?

SEAN. Sorry?

PATRICIA. I said what are you in for?

He looks perplexed.

Why are you here?

SEAN. Oh!

I like the sunshine.

He lifts his hand up into a sunbeam. She looks at him like he is mad, then smiles.

PATRICIA. The sunshine!

We hear the tea trolley again.

SEAN. Will you have tea?

PATRICIA. It's not actually here yet, Sean.

SEAN. Or cake? Dee brought cake.

PATRICIA. Did she?

SEAN. Yes.

PATRICIA. And who is Dee?

SEAN. Dee is my niece.

She's like her mother.

PATRICIA. Her mother?

SEAN. My sister, Pat.

Pat.

Short pause. Then confidentially.

I believe she's passed!

PATRICIA. Passed?

SEAN. Passed on!

PATRICIA. Oh… Dead… is it?

SEAN. Ahh yes.

PATRICIA. Well, isn't it well for Pat.

Not washed up in this place… or some hole like it.

SEAN. No. Indeed.

Slight pause.

Pat was always on the dot.

PATRICIA. Was she?

SEAN. I like that.

On the dot, and lovely.

PATRICIA. Good for Pat.

SEAN. Yes. Good for Pat.

Slight pause.

PATRICIA. So where's the other one then?

SEAN. Who?

PATRICIA. Dee?

SEAN. Ahhhhhh – she'll be with Matron.

PATRICIA. With Matron?

Why?

SEAN. They are… they are good friends, I believe.

PATRICIA. I see.

So you have friends on the inside!

SEAN. Have I?

PATRICIA. Handy that.

SEAN.…Excellent.

Pause.

PATRICIA. And what kind of cake is it?

SEAN. Oh! Please do…

He shakily proffers the box.

PATRICIA is impressed. She fixes her skirt on rising and takes the box to her chair.

PATRICIA. Thank you, Sean!

Oh… cream cornets!

SEAN. Yes.

PATRICIA. And I'm partial to a cream cornet!

SEAN. Excellent.

PATRICIA. There's nothing but sponge in this place!

A door upstage opens. The tea trolley is there. PATRICIA hops up too quickly. She feels a little wobble in her legs. The cakes drop. She stalls…

Oh dear. (*Grips the side of her chair.*)

SEAN. Oh my…

PATRICIA. It's all right. I'm fine.

SEAN. Might I assist? (*Attempts to rise.*)

PATRICIA. No. No. I'm absolutely fine

SEAN. Just a tick – (*As he gets to his feet.*)

PATRICIA. Please…

SEAN. We'll call!… Pull the cord!… SOS!

PATRICIA. I'm fine!

SEAN. Arms out!… Deep breath!

He reaches her.

PATRICIA. Jesus. I just jumped up.

SEAN. The lady's faint! SOS!

PATRICIA (*too quickly*)....Can you stop? Please.

   Please – stop, Sean.

SEAN. Stop...?

PATRICIA. I'm really... really... quite... fine.

SEAN. Are you?

PATRICIA. Yes.

   Yes. It's not... it's just... I got a 'start'.

SEAN. Oh, well... that's excellent.

PATRICIA. Thank you.

SEAN. No problem...

PATRICIA. It will pass. It passes quick.

SEAN. Does it?

PATRICIA. Yes... it's just a flurry... the heart... panic!

SEAN. Oh, I see.

PATRICIA....if I move too fast.

SEAN. Right.

PATRICIA. But it was so nice... so very nice of you... to stir...

SEAN. My pleasure.

PATRICIA. I'm fine now.

SEAN. Are you sure?

PATRICIA. Absolutely.

   He puts his hand on her face, like she was familiar to him.

SEAN. That's good...

PATRICIA (*startled by the physical contact*). Patricia!

SEAN. Patricia.

   He looks about for his wheelchair.

She indicates it. He smiles and shuffles back to sit.

She slowly lifts the cakes back to the table.

PATRICIA. I'll get our tea.

SEAN. The girl does it actually...

PATRICIA *is at the door.*

PATRICIA. How do you like yours?

SEAN. Oh! Yes please.

PATRICIA. With milk?

SEAN. Two lumps.

PATRICIA. Perfect.

SEAN. Thank you.

She gets two teas from beyond the door and returns to the room.

PATRICIA. Here we are!

SEAN. I am much obliged.

She settles in to her chair and opens the box again.

PATRICIA. No harm done!

SEAN. No harm done.

PATRICIA. Will you have the eclaire so?

SEAN. That would be lovely.

She passes it to him on a napkin and starts eating her cornet.

There is a nice silent sequence here. Eating, nodding, smiling.

PATRICIA. 'I would give all my fame for a pot of... tea'!

This is a conscious misquote from Shakespeare's Henry V. *It sparks a memory for* SEAN *who moves into a performance of the following speech. He starts hesitant and then builds.*

SEAN.

> 'Old men forget; yet all shall be forgot,
> But he'll remember with advantages
> What feats he did that day. Then shall our names,
> Familiar in his mouth as household words,
> Harry the King, Bedford, and Exeter,
> Warwick and Talbot, Salisbury and Gloucester,
> Be in their flowing cups freshly rememb'red.
> This story shall the good man teach his son;
> And Crispin Crispian shall ne'er go by,
> From this day to the ending of the world,
> But we in it shall be remembered
> We few, we happy few, we... we band of brothers;
> Shall...
> This story shall... shall think themselves... accursed...'

The performance was terrific, growing from hesitant to huge.
PATRICIA *is amazed and impressed...* SEAN *returns to his
eclaire.*

PATRICIA. My goodness!

SEAN. Henry the Fifth.

PATRICIA. I know.

SEAN. Many times.

PATRICIA. Many times what?

SEAN. Many times on the boards...

PATRICIA. You mean you played him?

SEAN. Henry Five...

PATRICIA. But that was excellent.

SEAN. Thank you.

PATRICIA. Excellent, Sean.

SEAN. He is one of my favourites actually.

PATRICIA. Is he?... So there's more?

SEAN. Many more.

PATRICIA. You're an actor!

SEAN. For my sins…

PATRICIA. Well! A cultured man… in this place!…

SEAN. Old men forget…

PATRICIA. I actually LOVE the theatre.

SEAN. Do you?

PATRICIA. Yes!

A regular audient.

SEAN. Well! Very good, very good.

PATRICIA. So might I have seen you?

He is lost.

Might I have seen you ON STAGE?

SEAN. 28 Haymarket, London SW.

PATRICIA. Is that a play?

SEAN. No, no. My agent.

PATRICIA. Goodness! A real actor.

Did you work in London?

SEAN. Oh yes.

PATRICIA. Imagine…?

SEAN. Predominently in film.

PATRICIA. Hah!

She can't believe it.

Sean Ceabhruill!

Well, of course – ?

I knew I knew that name!

SEAN. That's it.

PATRICIA. I am actually a teacher myself.

SEAN. Of course.

PATRICIA. Though I am retired two years.

SEAN (*makes a show of not believing her*). No… Never…?

PATRICIA. Oh! You are too kind, Sean Ceabhruill.

Primary.

Not as glamorous as stage and screen, obviously, but a good life.

SEAN. A wholesome life!

PATRICIA. YES!… yes…

Pause.

Oh, but you must miss it terribly?

SEAN.…What?

PATRICIA. The theatre…!

Your work

…Your life!

…I know I miss it.

SEAN *leans in confidentially. She leans in also.*

SEAN. I have some trouble with the words.

PATRICIA. Oh?

SEAN. Sometimes they stop.

PATRICIA. Do they?

SEAN. Disappear…

…Fade out.

PATRICIA. And have you tried carrots?

SEAN. What?

PATRICIA. They're good for the brain.

SEAN. Carrots?

PATRICIA. And walnuts.

And fish of course.

SEAN. Fish…?

PATRICIA. Yes. We must keep the brain active, Sean.

Play cards. Do crosswords.

'An active retirement and an active mind.'

That is my mantra – was my mantra.

That and peppermint tea, you see –

She knocks her head with her knuckle.

No dementia!

SEAN. Ahhhh.

Small pause.

I like cards.

PATRICIA. Do you, Sean?

SEAN. Poker!

PATRICIA. My favourite!

And are you a shark?

SEAN. No.

Tom's the shark.

PATRICIA. Who's Tom?

SEAN. The shark!

She laughs.

PATRICIA. Well, we'll have to play!

SEAN. Why not?

PATRICIA. I'll get a pack.

SEAN. There's the pack in the cabinet.

PATRICIA. What cabinet?

SEAN. And I'll have a gin.

PATRICIA. A gin?

SEAN. I'm fond of a gin.

PATRICIA. Who isn't…?

SEAN. Shall we have the Cusacks round?

PATRICIA. The Cusacks?… Let's!

SEAN. Give them a bell and I'll do nibbles.

PATRICIA. Gorgeous!

And how about Gregory Peck?!

SEAN. Is he in town?

PATRICIA. Hah! I love it!

He tries to get up.

SEAN. I can't seem to find my feet?

PATRICIA. But they're right there, Sean.

In your slippers.

SEAN. In my slippers?

I'm in my…

PATRICIA. Slippers.

SEAN. Why?

PATRICIA. I don't quite know.

SEAN. Tom?

PATRICIA. No?

SEAN. No, no.

PATRICIA. It's me, Patricia. We're playing… well, we were about to play cards.

SEAN. Were we?

PATRICIA. Yes.

I think so.

SEAN. Where am I?

PATRICIA. You're in the conservatory.

SEAN. Nonsense. We don't have a conservatory.

Where's Tom?

PATRICIA. I don't know Tom.

SEAN. I'd like to see him.

PATRICIA. Well…?

SEAN. Why is he never home!

He pauses.

He looks at her as if for the first time.

Excuse me… I… I!

PATRICIA. I think you're a little confused.

SEAN. Yes.

I think… I seem… I think I feel quite tired.

PATRICIA. Oh, of course.

SEAN. Can you…?

Do you think you might pull… ring…

He indicates the bell-cord which has become tangled and just out of reach.

PATRICIA. Yes. Of course, of course I can.

She pulls the bell for him.

SEAN. Thank you.

PATRICIA. No problem.

SEAN. The nurse will come.

PATRICIA. Yes!

SEAN. The nurse comes.

PATRICIA. Really?

I'm not so sure in this place.

The door upstage opens.

SEAN. Ah!

He goes to rise.

Good day!

End of scene.

Scene Two

PATRICIA *enters the conservatory with a CD player in her hand. Her hair is different – the lipstick obvious.*

PATRICIA. Ahh, there you are!

SEAN (*goes to rise*). Good day!

PATRICIA. The nurse spirited you away after breakfast?

SEAN. Yes.

PATRICIA. No head for chess, I presume?

SEAN. I… I take a rest.

PATRICIA. Really? From what?

SEAN. I don't know exactly…?

PATRICIA. Well… I thought you might like some music?

SEAN. Music!

PATRICIA. Yes.

I know I can't imagine the day without it.

And all they blare out there is television!

SEAN. Ghastly.

PATRICIA. Agreed…

So will I try it?

SEAN. Oh… do… yes please.

She plugs in the CD player.

PATRICIA. Is there no one else uses this place?

SEAN. Ah… not really

…it's a tad drafty.

PATRICIA. Except for the hardy buck!

SEAN. Ha! The hardy buck!

The music starts. It is the classic theme to Love Story *by Henry Mancini.*

PATRICIA. There!

They listen. She wobbles the player quite violently.

The sound's not great but '*quelle surprise*' in this place.

SEAN. No… no. That's wonderfu…

PATRICIA. Is it wonderful?!

She is pleased.

I thought you'd be a man for the classics.

… This is *Classics on Film*!

SEAN. Excellent.

He starts conducting the music in the air.

They listen to the music.

PATRICIA. I'll admit it! I googled you up, Sean!

SEAN. Did you?

PATRICIA. Sure there were a thousand hits!

SEAN. Really?

PATRICIA. You've had quite the career!...

SEAN. Who had?

PATRICIA. Ustinov!... Hepburn!... Caine!

(*Impressed*.)...I mean, Michael Caine!

SEAN (*imitates Michael Caine*). 'It's a very difficult job and the only way to get through it is we all work together as a team. And that means you do everything I say.'

PATRICIA (*applauds*). Oh, fabulous, that's fabulous, Sean.

SEAN. The... I... I... *Italian Job*.

PATRICIA. Of course.

Do you know they should put you in the brochure!

SEAN. Sorry?

PATRICIA. For this place!... I mean, I'm surprised moneybags hasn't thought of it... you'd draw in more clients than the incontinence chairs...

SEAN. Would I?

PATRICIA. I was just saying that to Nora...

SEAN. Nora?

PATRICIA. My sister.

'Sean Ceabhruill' I said.

And sure she knew you right off!

SEAN. Your sister?

PATRICIA. On the phone!

SEAN. Ah.

PATRICIA. And that's amazing for Nora –

She wondered actually, if you really got to Rome?

SEAN. If I got to Rome?

PATRICIA. For the film?

With Mrs Ceabhruill?

SEAN. With who?

PATRICIA. But I said that wasn't likely.

SEAN. What wasn't likely?

PATRICIA. They probably don't like relatives on set?

SEAN. Who?

PATRICIA. Or does she not travel?

SEAN. Who?

PATRICIA. Mrs Ceabhruill?

SEAN. Who is this Mrs Ceabhruill?

PATRICIA. Your wife!

SEAN. But I don't have a wife.

PATRICIA. Don't you?

SEAN. No. Never.

PATRICIA. Well…! My goodness…!

And Rome so romantic a city.

SEAN. Is it?

PATRICIA. Isn't it?

SEAN. I suppose.

The music sticks. She gives it a belt, SEAN *is startled. The CD leaps to the next tune, the theme from* Doctor Zhivago.

PATRICIA. Oh!

Oh no. I don't think I'm able for this one…

SEAN. Why not?

PATRICIA. Don't you know it?

SEAN *makes a show of listening*.

SEAN. It's Jarre… Genius!

PATRICIA. Who could ever get over Omar?

Will you ever forget him… in his hat?!

SEAN. Indeed…

PATRICIA. You see they knew how to make films back then didn't they, Sean…

SEAN. They did.

PATRICIA. Not like the current muck.

SEAN. No.

They listen.

SEAN *is moving his foot to the music*.

PATRICIA. What on earth are you doing in that wheelchair?

SEAN. Hah?

PATRICIA. Just look at your foot!

He looks at his foot, as if it is not part of him, as if it is misbehaving.

SEAN.…It's just for transport!

PATRICIA. You can't give up, Sean.

Don't you know that. We must never give up!

She is upon him.

Here!

Take my right arm.

SEAN. What's happening...?

PATRICIA. Right arm!

SEAN. Oh righty-oh.

PATRICIA. Don't worry – I have all the moves.

SEAN. Do you?!

She hauls him up. He is delighted.

PATRICIA. I did the soup run with Simon for years. Hauled more drunks from their sleeping bags than you've had BAFTAs. Upsadaisy.

SEAN. Marvellous.

He is standing.

Oh!

He looks at her, standing right next to him.

Shall we dance?

PATRICIA. Dance?

He takes up the pose of a man about to waltz but his arm is not around her waist but around fresh air...

Why not?

I can see that there's nothing wrong with those legs!

SEAN (*looks down at them*). A tad slow...

PATRICIA. So take a step!

SEAN. Take a step?

She takes an exaggerated step. He watches, then he takes a step. She takes a step. And he takes a step. He is quite enjoying it.

PATRICIA. I knew it.

All you need is a stick!

SEAN. I had a good stick.

PATRICIA. Give that leg a stretch!

SEAN. In what manner?

PATRICIA. Like this.

She stretches her leg behind her.

Here! Put your hands on your hips.

SEAN. Oh.

PATRICIA (*starts to manipulate his arms*). On your hips!

SEAN. Got it! Got it!

PATRICIA. Good.

Now – (*Demonstrates.*)

Stretch the left leg back.

He does so.

Feel the stretch! Is that taut?

SEAN. Yes.

PATRICIA. Excellent… and back to base.

He returns his leg.

Next one!

Stretch!

Very good.

Now, how are the knees?

He is still standing hands on hips.

SEAN. Two knees!

PATRICIA. Excellent.

She demonstrates bending the knees gently.

The music now changes to The King and I.

Up and down. Up and down.

SEAN follows the knee-bending exercise, then puts out his foot and taps.

Oh!

Do you actully dance, Sean?

SEAN. Not my forte.

Though I took to the floor in *The King and I*.

He does three tentative steps again and adopts the pose for a polka.

One two three. One two three.

PATRICIA. But that's excellent.

He then starts to adopt a Yul Brynner accent as he moves into The King And I *'Shall We Dance' sequence.*

SEAN. One two three. One two three.

Then to PATRICIA, *as if she is the other character.*

Stop! You have made me lose my count.

PATRICIA. Have I?

He takes PATRICIA*'s two hands forcefully.*

SEAN. Again!

He leads her in a dance, focusing on his feet.

One two three. One two three.

PATRICIA. See! You're full of surprises.

He joggles her.

SEAN. 'But this is not how I will see the Europeans dance tonight?'

PATRICIA. Isn't it?

He now puts his arm around PATRICIA*'s waist and takes her hand as if for a dance.*

SEAN (*forceful and in character*). Come!

PATRICIA. Oh my goodness.

They both attempt a very very slow dance.

But this is extraordinary.

SEAN (*sings to the music*). Bumtedabum... Bumtedabum.

The CD starts to stick again and SEAN *sticks with his bumtedabum and dance. So* PATRICIA *disengages and goes to change the CD.*

PATRICIA. Hang on. I have another disc...

She goes over to the CD player and starts to go through the discs, talking with her back to him. He is still attempting to dance.

I asked that matron for a device, 'I keep all my music on iPod,' I told her. 'What I need is the dock... don't you have one?... A dock?... A speaker thing!?' I might as well have been speaking Swahili.

SEAN *is still in the middle of the floor, dancing and then stalling as the music sticks. He is stranded when the music stops.*

I don't know where they do their training! Anyway it was one of the foreign hands came up with this – (*The CD.*) A man-nurse – looks Korean. I like him best I think – he has less to say.

Mozart!

SEAN *remains stranded in the middle of the floor. Not a notion what he is doing there.*

Sean?

SEAN. Yes?

PATRICIA. The man-nurse brought some Mozart.

SEAN. Wonderful.

PATRICIA *sits.*

I might just sit down...?

PATRICIA. Do.

> SEAN *realises she is not going to help him back to the chair and so tentatively makes his own way back.*

> You don't need that wheelchair.

> You have two good legs.

SEAN. I do.

> Good ploughing legs.

PATRICIA. Ploughing?

SEAN (*as he sits*). Abbeydorney Champion 1958.

PATRICIA. Were you really...?

SEAN. No. No. My father. James John Ceabhruill.

PATRICIA. Your father was a farmer then?

SEAN. That's it.

> Sixty-five acres.

PATRICIA. Lovely.

SEAN. Front yard to Grady's gate.

PATRICIA. My own people were farmers!

SEAN. Is that so...

PATRICIA. Something else we have in common...

SEAN. Superb.

PATRICIA. My daddy was on the farm... before he came to Dublin...

SEAN. How many fields?

PATRICIA. How many fields?

SEAN. Yes.

PATRICIA. I'm afraid I've no idea. I can't say I took an interest. I was more the academic.

SEAN. Ahhhhh.

PATRICIA. Books, poetry... plays!

SEAN. Cattle?

PATRICIA. I couldn't tell you.

SEAN. Nine fields!

PATRICIA. Nine fields?

Oh... in Nenagh is it?

SEAN. There was Clancy's Field...

Hay Field.

The Callows.

Castle Hill.

Railway.

Split Hill.

Bailey's Gate.

Louie's.

The Inch.

...and home.

PATRICIA. Really...

SEAN. Potatoes. Cattle. Oats.

PATRICIA. So who's there now?

SEAN. Who's there now?

PATRICIA. Yes.

No response.

Don't you visit?

Would you not like to visit?

SEAN. I'd like to visit…

PATRICIA. And so you should.

We are not incarcerated, you know.

Ask your Dee to take you.

SEAN. Or down on the scooter!

Vroooom vroooooom.

PATRICIA. You're gas…

SEAN. Feel the sun through the jumper.

Have a pint at The Tap.

And then Mammy's table.

Glorious.

Slight pause.

Glorious days.

PATRICIA. They sound it…

SEAN. Gone!

PATRICIA. Why do you say that?

SEAN. Well, Mammy's gone.

The fields are gone…

She is uncomfortable.

PATRICIA. But there's something else… there's always something else isn't there. You mentioned Rathmines?

SEAN. Gone too.

PATRICIA. How can it be gone?

Have you sold it?

SEAN. No. No.

PATRICIA. So who's living there?

Who's minding it?

No response.

Do you never go home, Sean?

SEAN. No one goes home.

PATRICIA. What?

SEAN. No one goes home from here.

PATRICIA. Nonsense.

SEAN. No...

PATRICIA. Well, I'll tell you – I intend to.

SEAN. Why?

PATRICIA. Because... because I have a life, of course!...
    Because I can't just sit here and go gaga. I mean, is that it,
    Sean?... Is that the grand plan?

SEAN. I don't know really...

PATRICIA (*forcefully*). I am just here on respite.

SEAN. Is that a fact?

PATRICIA. Yes, that's a fact.

    I am here for a rest.

    For a period.

SEAN. I see.

PATRICIA. I still have a home!

SEAN. And family...?

PATRICIA (*increasingly irritated*). Yes. Well, Nora. My sister.
    She's my family.

    We live together.

SEAN. Do you?

PATRICIA. Yes.

SEAN. Company!

PATRICIA. Yes.

Pause.

SEAN. So why are you here?

PATRICIA. Because… because I have some medical issues.

SEAN. Medical issues?

PATRICIA. Yes.

SEAN. Is it terminal?

PATRICIA. Jesus, no.

SEAN. It's usually terminal.

PATRICIA. Well, this isn't.

SEAN. Is it cancer?

PATRICIA. No it's not cancer thank you very much.

It's the liver if you must know.

SEAN. Ahh!

PATRICIA. Sclerosis.

SEAN. Yes.

PATRICIA. What do you mean, yes?

SEAN. I…

PATRICIA. What?

It's not from drink if that's what you're thinking?! Why does everyone think it's from drink…?

SEAN. I didn't…

PATRICIA. I can see you… I can just see you thinking… and it's infuriating.

SEAN. …I just suppose in most cases.

PATRICIA. BUT not in mine, thank you.

I live my life in moderation.

SEAN. Do you?

PATRICIA. Yes.

None of the excess of a movie star I'd imagine…

SEAN. Excellent.

PATRICIA. Yes it is excellent.

It's all excellent because I haven't had a fit since I came here!

SEAN. Well… well done!

PATRICIA. Thank you.

Slight pause.

SEAN. And what is a fit?

PATRICIA. I don't really want to go in to it…

SEAN. What's that…?

PATRICIA. I said I don't really want to… (*Sighs.*) It's a seizure… a type of a blackout.

SEAN. Oh dear…

PATRICIA. There's a flow from the liver or something and it stops.

SEAN. Dreadful!

PATRICIA. Well, it can be.

SEAN. Like a faint?

PATRICIA. Sort of… only rigid… more a stroke.

SEAN. God!

PATRICIA. I feel a heat…

SEAN. Do you?

PATRICIA. Yes. And then it's hard to breathe. And everything goes dark, if it's a fit… but sometimes it isn't. It's a false alarm!

SEAN. Is it?

PATRICIA. If I'm anxious.

SEAN. I see... (*He doesn't!*)

PATRICIA. But if I go, if I really go... out cold, you know and into the darkness. Well, then I can't remember.

SEAN. Ah! I know that...

PATRICIA. Know what?

SEAN. To not remember.

PATRICIA. Yes.

But this is quite manageable.

SEAN. Is it?

PATRICIA. Of course.

SEAN. For Nora?

PATRICIA. No not for Nora. Not right now... but it will be. When we find the right tablets.

SEAN. Ahhhh.

PATRICIA. She just needed a break. We needed a break because she's not always able.

SEAN. Of course.

PATRICIA. It's been quite distressing actually...

SEAN. I'm sorry.

PATRICIA. But I'm fine. I will be fine. When I go home. After this rest.

SEAN. Well, I'm delighted.

PATRICIA. Good.

Pause.

SEAN. I might miss you though.

PATRICIA. What?

SEAN. If you go!

PATRICIA. Oh...

Slight pause.

I suppose I might miss you too.

They both sit quietly listening to the music.

End of scene.

Scene Three

PATRICIA *is well dressed. She is looking out through the patio doors – she is waiting. The upstage door opens and* SEAN *appears in the doorway on a walker.*

SEAN. Ta-dah!

PATRICIA. Well, look at you!

SEAN (*talking to himself as he walks into the room and toward* PATRICIA). Keep it up. Keep it up!

PATRICIA. Why, that's wonderful, Sean!

Who got you the walker?

SEAN. Man-nurse.

PATRICIA. I told you he's the best of them.

SEAN. And I just met Matron.

'Ten out of ten,' she said, 'Ten out of ten.'

PATRICIA. Well, she ought to be sued. She has half the inmates drugged and the other half in wheelchairs.

SEAN. Is it Sunday?

PATRICIA. I think you know well it's Sunday.

SEAN. I hope we've not missed the roast chicken?

PATRICIA. That's not till two.

SEAN. Ah! Plenty of time.

PATRICIA. We're up at six, there's always plenty of time.

SEAN. Roast chicken is my favourite.

PATRICIA. I know.

He joins her and lets go of the walker and with his two hands –

SEAN. Ta-dah!

PATRICIA (*laughs*).... You look smart.

SEAN. Thank you.

Perhaps it's the necktie?

PATRICIA. I noticed the necktie.

SEAN. Good.

Purple for the lupin.

Lupinus lupin.

I can see them from my window.

PATRICIA. And from here.

SEAN. On this beautiful day!

PATRICIA. 'Here's flowers for you'! (*From* The Winter's Tale.)

SEAN. Ahh, yes!

He pulls a plastic flower from his inside pocket and gives it to her.

'Here's flowers for you!

... these are flowers
Of middle summer, and I think they are given
To men of middle age.'

He gives her a little bow.

PATRICIA. Oh!

Well!

Thank you!

SEAN. Not at all.

(*Conspiratorially*.) Fresh from the hall stand!

PATRICIA *laughs but is quite overcome by this. She blurts out…*

PATRICIA. I used to teach that verse.

SEAN. Did you?

PATRICIA. Yes.

To sixth class!

SEAN. Excellent.

PATRICIA. Yes.

SEAN *is right beside her.*

She is quite conscious of his proximity.

She looks straight ahead.

And it is a beautiful day!

SEAN (*leans right into her*). Halcyon!

They hold each other's eyes a fraction too long and then both turn away and look straight out into the garden.

Pause.

He pulls at his collar a little to loosen it.

She glances at him.

They're not so easy to manage – neckties!

PATRICIA. No?

SEAN. Even the fingers forget!

PATRICIA (*coquettish*). So you should have asked Matron!

SEAN. I did actually.

And she obliged.

PATRICIA. Oh, did she now!

There is another slight pause as the mention of Matron has soured the moment. They still stand side by side.

SEAN. Are we waiting for someone?

PATRICIA. I am waiting for Nora.

SEAN. Oh, of course.

PATRICIA. She's on the bus.

SEAN. Is she?! Well, we must get biscuits!

PATRICIA. No, I mean she's on the bus in that she gets the bus, I'm not sure if she's on the bus right now.

SEAN. Oh!

And is it a long journey?

PATRICIA. Well, yes, when you're on the bus.

This place is in the middle of nowhere.

SEAN. Is it?

PATRICIA. Yes.

SEAN. And not too many buses to nowhere!

PATRICIA. No, Sean.

Not too many buses to nowhere.

Pause. She shifts as if to move away but SEAN *interrupts her…*

SEAN. Dee drives! She parks by the side door.

PATRICIA. I know she does.

SEAN. Doesn't Nora drive?

PATRICIA. No. Nora lives on her nerves.

Pause.

Again she goes to move away but SEAN *gently puts his hand on her arm.*

SEAN. Will you still come to see me when you're out?

PATRICIA. Oh, of course I will!

Of course I will, Sean.

SEAN. That's good.

He looks at her. He seems so vulnerable. She comforts him…

PATRICIA. We could go for a spin!

SEAN. A jaunt!

PATRICIA. Exactly.

SEAN. Marvellous! And where will we go?

PATRICIA. Well, where would you like to go?

SEAN. To the sea!

PATRICIA. The sea?

SEAN. Yes.

PATRICIA. Do you like the sea?

SEAN. I love it.

I swim every day.

I mean… I used to swim every day.

PATRICIA. Really?

SEAN. At Rathmines Baths.

PATRICIA. But that's not the sea!

SEAN. Near enough.

PATRICIA. You never said…

SEAN. Didn't I?

PATRICIA. No.

SEAN (*moves right in again and whispers*). You might find
there's a lot you don't know about Sean Ceabhruill!

*There is a moment. They are face to face. She gently leans
forward and kisses him. He stands frozen. She becomes more
passionate and embraces him.*

He pulls away – gagging.

Good God!

PATRICIA. What?

SEAN. SOS.

PATRICIA. What?

SEAN. What was that about?

PATRICIA. I'm just… I'm sorry… didn't you want it?

SEAN. Want it!… Jesus… And tongue!

PATRICIA. What?

SEAN. You used your tongue!

PATRICIA. I didn't.

SEAN. You did. I felt it flipping around in there.

PATRICIA. Please…

SEAN. You're disgusting.

PATRICIA. You're disgusting!

SEAN. What made you?… How could you?…

PATRICIA. it's…

It was…

…It's just a kiss.

SEAN. But from you!

PATRICIA. What's wrong with me?

SEAN. You're old!

PATRICIA. I am younger than you!

SEAN. You're a woman!

PATRICIA. Of course I'm a woman.

SEAN. My God!

Why is it always the same with you?

PATRICIA. With who?

SEAN. With a woman!

…Show them a bit of attention and they're off!

PATRICIA. What?

SEAN. I've had it all my life…

PATRICIA. What?

SEAN. With your hands and your lacquer and your lipstick!

And I've no interest. I'm not interested.

PATRICIA. RIGHT. I get it…

SEAN. You always misconstrue…?

PATRICIA. What is there to misconstrue?… YOU!… Poncing around with your Lupinus lupin…?

SEAN. Stop!

PATRICIA. You're mad for it!

SEAN. My God you're deranged.

PATRICIA. I bet you're one of those repressed…

SEAN. There's nothing… dep… rep… dep…

PATRICIA. Repressed!

SEAN. Exactly. About me!

PATRICIA. But you started it?

SEAN. I did not start it.

PATRICIA. You did. With your flower… and your poetry!

SEAN. That was YOUR poetry!

PATRICIA. No it wasn't.

SEAN. It was!!!!!!

PATRICIA. So GET out then.

SEAN. Don't worry I'm going.

PATRICIA. Get up on your walker and go!

SEAN. I'm gone!

PATRICIA. Just leave me alone.

SEAN. This is as fast as I go!

PATRICIA. You bastard.

SEAN. I'm sorry.

PATRICIA. You bastard!

SEAN. Oh, please, stop saying that.

PATRICIA. You led me on.

SEAN. I didn't.

I had no intention…

PATRICIA. I think you did.

SEAN. No.

I like you… that's all.

I enjoy you.

I thought we were friends.

PATRICIA. And so did I…

SEAN. No one talks to me.

No one listens to me.

Not for years.

PATRICIA. Because you're cruel.

SEAN. I don't want to be cruel.

   Please… Patricia.

PATRICIA. No. No. I'm mortified.

SEAN. So am I really.

   Slight pause.

   Maybe we can walk round it… or better still forget it?!

PATRICIA. But why don't you want to be kissed?

SEAN. I'm sorry.

PATRICIA. Why?

SEAN. Because…

PATRICIA. Because what?

SEAN. Because I'm finished with all that.

PATRICIA. Why?

SEAN. Because I was never any good at it.

PATRICIA. But you must have had loads of sex in the movies.

SEAN. I wasn't in the movies!

PATRICIA. I looked you up.

SEAN. BIT PARTS!

PATRICIA. I thought everyone liked to be kissed.

SEAN. Not me.

PATRICIA. But why?

SEAN. Oh, what does it matter?

PATRICIA. It matters to me.

   Slight pause.

SEAN. Because I love someone.

PATRICIA. You love someone?

SEAN. Yes.

PATRICIA. Who?

Who do you love?

SEAN....I love Tom.

PATRICIA. Tom?

SEAN. Yes.

PATRICIA. Who's Tom?

SEAN. Tom is… well, Tom is Tom.

PATRICIA. Is he your son?

SEAN. No. No. No.

I don't have a son.

PATRICIA. So who is he?

SEAN. He's my partner.

PATRICIA. Your what?

SEAN. My partner.

My lover.

My friend.

PATRICIA. Dear God!

SEAN. I'm sorry.

PATRICIA. No!

No…

SEAN. I'm terribly sorry.

PATRICIA. Please! Don't be.

SEAN. Do you think we could stop this now… I feel. I think I feel quite tired.

PATRICIA. You're tired?

SEAN. Yes.

PATRICIA. Oh, I see…

SEAN. I'm sorry.

PATRICIA. What is it you're so sorry about?

SEAN. I think I've upset you.

PATRICIA. Well, you haven't upset me.

Surprised me maybe…?

SEAN. I think you're a beautiful woman, Patricia.

PATRICIA. Oh, please!

SEAN. I do!

PATRICIA. But you're a gay!

SEAN. I'm not 'a' anything.

PATRICIA. You are!

And you should have told me.

You should have said.

SEAN. But why?

How?

PATRICIA. You just should have!

SEAN. I'm sorry.

PATRICIA. And will you stop BEING sorry.

SEAN. Yes… Yes.

Pause.

It's just… I'm just…

Don't you have someone?

PATRICIA. Don't I what?

SEAN. A boyfriend?

PATRICIA. A boyfriend?

SEAN. A lover?

PATRICIA. Tucked into my locker, Sean?

Under my bed?

Jesus! Don't you think you'd know that by now?

It's me and Nora... Isn't it? I suppose it's always been me and Nora and if I had someone else, I would have said.

SEAN. Always?

PATRICIA. Well, maybe not always...

...But recent. Yes. In more recent times.

SEAN. Why?

PATRICIA. I don't know why.

SEAN. Oh!

PATRICIA. I suppose I've been busy.

SEAN. You've been busy?

PATRICIA. Yes. Busy.

I've had my career!

SEAN. Ah yes...

PATRICIA. I was twenty years a principal!

SEAN. Of course.

PATRICIA. Near two thousand children have passed through these hands.

She looks at her hands.

SEAN. Have they?

PATRICIA. Yes.

She wrings her hands.

So I suppose. I think. I mean, I THINK I didn't have time.

SEAN. It can be hard to make time.

PATRICIA. Yes. Exactly. It can be hard to make time and I
    didn't... that's it, in my head, or in my body, make time for
    anyone else.

SEAN. Oh!

I'm sorry.

PATRICIA. Yes. Me too.

I mean... yes... I think that's what I mean. I'm sorry now
too... because I'm near the end.

I'm at the end, Sean.

*He looks at her. He reaches for her hand but she recoils from
him.*

Please!

Slight pause.

I suppose we all don't get it all.

Do we, Sean?

We all don't get that perfect life.

The door upstage opens. They both turn.

PATRICIA *steadies herself.*

I would imagine that's your Dee.

End of scene.

Scene Four

PATRICIA *is on a small bench outside the conservatory, just next to the sliding door. We can see inside. The cake box is on the table but no Dee handbag. The upstage door opens and* SEAN *enters on his walker. He expects to see* PATRICIA. *He is surprised to see her outside. He raises his hand but she has her back to him. He makes his way up to the doors. He knocks on the glass.* PATRICIA *looks around. He waves. She waves and turns back into the sun.* SEAN *hovers. He knocks again on the window. He mouths something. She waves again. He is disconcerted. He goes to sit on his chair inside. He keeps turning to look out at* PATRICIA. PATRICIA *takes a handkerchief from her bag and wipes her nose.* SEAN *is watching ardently from inside. He rises again and comes to the doors. He knocks on the doors. She turns again. He mimes that she open the door so she gets up and struggles to get it open. He stands inside on his walker. She sits back down again outside.*

SEAN. Hello!

PATRICIA....Hello.

SEAN. It's nice and sunny out there.

PATRICIA. Yes it is.

    Pause.

SEAN. You didn't come to lunch?

PATRICIA. I wasn't hungry.

SEAN. Not like you!

PATRICIA. No.

SEAN. I kept you cake...

    The c... cornet!

PATRICIA. I'm still not hungry.

Pause.

SEAN. So how was your visit?

No response.

How was...?

PATRICIA. Nora.

SEAN. That's it... Nora.

PATRICIA. She couldn't come.

SEAN. Oh dear.

PATRICIA. Yes.

SEAN. Is she ill?

PATRICIA. No.

She's stressed.

Distressed.

SEAN. I'm sorry.

PATRICIA. Well...

SEAN. What?

PATRICIA. Nothing.

SEAN. I'm sorry, I can't quite hear you!

PATRICIA. So why the hell don't you come outside?

Slight pause.

He is standing lost in the doorway.

SEAN. I don't actually come outside!

PATRICIA. What?

SEAN. I don't...

PATRICIA. I know, I heard you, but why?

SEAN. Because… I don't know really.

PATRICIA. Well, it's beautiful.

SEAN. Is it?

PATRICIA. Do you want to come outside?

SEAN. Yes actually…

PATRICIA. So come on then!

He is a bit baffled but eventually lifts his walker out through the door, inching himself just beyond it.

SEAN. Oh, oh my goodness. It's warm.

PATRICIA. Isn't it.

SEAN. And I can feel it.

On my face.

PATRICIA. Yes.

SEAN. I can feel the day.

PATRICIA. Yes.

Pause as he soaks it up.

I suppose you want to sit down now?

SEAN. May I?

PATRICIA.…I'll hoosh up.

He sits down next to her and gently pushes his walker to his right.

She is careful not to touch him. They are silent.

There is the sound of a car taking off. SEAN *waves.*

SEAN. It's Dee… leaving.

PATRICIA. I know.

SEAN. She will wonder why I'm out here.

PATRICIA. Will she?

SEAN. Perhaps.

PATRICIA. Why does she even come?

SEAN. Sorry?

PATRICIA. She barely speaks to you.

A quick peck, then she drops her bag and goes.

SEAN. She used to speak to me.

PATRICIA. Really?

SEAN. I think she just got tired of it.

But she's a good girl, Dee…

PATRICIA *watches her go*.

PATRICIA. You can see the dread, can't you, on every visiting face.

Pause.

SEAN. Why not enjoy the sunshine?

PATRICIA. I'm not in the form.

Pause.

SEAN. Do you sit in your garden at home?

PATRICIA. Of course.

Under my lilac.

SEAN. I like a lilac!

PATRICIA. This one was planted the day I moved in.

SEAN. How lovely.

PATRICIA. With lavender… and roses.

SEAN. Fragrant!

PATRICIA. Exactly.

SEAN. So you have a spot?

PATRICIA. I do.

I love my spot.

SEAN. Of course.

PATRICIA. I sit there for hours…

SEAN. Lovely.

PATRICIA. With a good book.

SEAN. That's it.

PATRICIA. Though I would usually take my top off!

He looks aghast.

Relax!… It's just to get the sun in my bones… but like everything, Sean, I am not at home, I'm here; where even the simplest pleasure can cause a riot!

She takes out her handkerchief again and wipes her nose.

SEAN. Well, maybe you should do as you please?

PATRICIA. Do you think so?

SEAN. To quote a dear friend

'We are not incarcerated'!

PATRICIA. That's me?!

SEAN. Is it?

PATRICIA. You are quoting me now?

SEAN. Am I?… I get confused…

PATRICIA. I don't believe you do!

But sod it!

She takes off her top. She is in her bra.

There!

Any swooners?

SEAN (*looks around*). Dan Brennan looks a bit shaky.

PATRICIA. They're all a bit shaky in this place.

SEAN *sneaks a side look at her.*

SEAN. Very nice.

PATRICIA *laughs heartily.*

PATRICIA. I thought you weren't interested!

SEAN. It looks liberating!

PATRICIA. So why don't you join me?

SEAN. I don't think I would manage my buttons!

PATRICIA. God help us!

She laughs again.

Pause.

What am I going to do, Sean?

SEAN. About what?

PATRICIA. About everything.

It's such a mess.

SEAN. What's a mess?

PATRICIA. Everything.

Nora says we might have to sell our house.

SEAN. What?

PATRICIA. Our house!

I can't believe it.

And I can't believe I can't believe it.

What on earth was I thinking? Our home, Sean!

SEAN. But why?

PATRICIA. To pay for this place! It costs a fortune. A fortune, Sean!

You must know that?

She wipes a tear.

SEAN. Oh dear… (*Fumbles with a handkerchief.*)

PATRICIA. And what kills me is the waste!

> And I've said it to that matron, 'What are we paying for? I mean, there's not a one here that will turn out the lights! And then the doors are left wide open and there's too much food on our plates.'

SEAN. And what did she say?

PATRICIA (*sighs*). She just warned me not to get overwrought!

SEAN. So perhaps you shouldn't get overwrought.

PATRICIA. Just whose side are you on?

SEAN. I don't want anything to happen to you, Patricia.

PATRICIA. But something is happening.

> Something is happening, Sean, and I feel like I'm losing…

> Everything that matters.

> *Short pause.*

> I should never have come here.

> We can't afford it.

> And the truth is we were managing fine.

> Until the last one.

SEAN. Last what?

PATRICIA. Stroke! Episode! Fit! Whatever you want to call it.

> This cursed affliction that's eating me up.

> I mean there I was; folding clothes. Just folding clothes on the landing when I started to feel it coming, the heat… and then I thought I grabbed the banister… but when they found me, I was apparently twisted at the foot of the stair. I can't remember a thing but poor Nora! She said she could see me through the front glass… but couldn't force open the door.

> There were ambulances… and a fire brigade… dear Jesus, such a ridiculous fuss!

SEAN. But you could have been killed!

PATRICIA. And would that have been such a bad thing?

Would it, Sean?

When I see to what we're reduced!

Short pause.

SEAN. Some people are happy here.

PATRICIA. I don't believe that. Not for a minute.

Are you happy?

SEAN. I'm more –

I'm more finished.

PATRICIA. But why?

SEAN. It's easier that way.

Pause.

PATRICIA. Is it because of Tom?

No response.

Where is he, Sean?

SEAN. I think I'd rather not... if you don't mind, Patricia.

PATRICIA. I've never seen him?

SEAN. Not talk about Tom.

PATRICIA. But where does he live?

Is he in Rathmines?

SEAN. Yes, he's in Rathmines.

PATRICIA. In your house?

SEAN. Our house, his house, what does it matter?

PATRICIA. Is it his house?

SEAN. No!

No it's not.

PATRICIA. So why don't I see him?

SEAN. I don't know.

PATRICIA. Does he visit?

Does he visit, Sean?

SEAN. NO.

No. no.

…He used to visit.

PATRICIA. So why did he stop?

When did he stop?

SEAN. I don't know.

PATRICIA. And you love him?

SEAN. Yes I love him.

This isn't his life.

PATRICIA. But aren't you his life? His partner?

SEAN. Please…

PATRICIA. I'm sorry I don't understand.

I don't understand anything any more.

Slight pause.

SEAN. He's a good man.

PATRICIA. A good man would be here.

SEAN. No.

Everything changed…

PATRICIA. How? How did everything change?

SEAN. He was… He is… he's a beautiful man, Patricia.

Charming and quick. The centre of every room, every event, that's Tom. And we were happy, yes, incredibly happy… for many years. Our house was full… so full, Patricia… of every life and every wish… and parties, there were lots of parties… but then… I got old.

PATRICIA. We all get old.

SEAN. Not Tom.

And then the world turned... didn't it? Just a tad. And I missed it, I seemed to miss it somehow... because suddenly there were new bars, in Dublin at any rate... and clubs...

PATRICIA. You go to clubs?

SEAN. No! No, no. Not me. That's it, you see. I'm too old-fashioned.

PATRICIA. You've got more sense.

SEAN. Have I?

I don't know.

Because then I lost him, didn't I? Lost Tom... lost something... because we were...? we were...? no longer in sync! – yes, that's it, 'synchronised', because I wanted, you see, and he didn't. What did I want? I wanted... peace, yes, peace, by the fireside. Just the two of us. Because he was enough for me.

And I started... I started forgetting. Like an old man. Little things, just little things; dates, events. It was almost amusing, endearing... but then... well, it was difficult, it is difficult for Tom.

PATRICIA. Why?

SEAN. Because!... Patricia.

PATRICIA. Because what?

SEAN. He tried. We both tried. To mop it up! To fasten! To fasten our lives unravelling because he loved it too, loved me too. But I was stupid, I wouldn't concede... I tried to pretend and then in company, well, you see; disorientated! I might try use the phone to change the television or put the cups away in the fridge or find a toilet in quite the wrong place...

He couldn't stand it. I couldn't stand it. I became decrepit in his eyes.

PATRICIA. The bastard!

SEAN. No. No.

PATRICIA. He's obviously a bastard!

SEAN. I think I'd like to go inside...

He starts to get up.

PATRICIA. He just deserted you!

SEAN. No.

It makes sense, Patricia. I am useless now.

He struggles with the walker.

PATRICIA. You are not useless.

SEAN. Please...

PATRICIA. He doesn't deserve you, Sean!

SEAN. I need to go inside.

He is trying to turn the walker.

Will you...? Can you...?

PATRICIA. Okay... okay I'll get it.

SEAN. And open the door.

PATRICIA. It's already open.

SEAN. It might be SOS.

PATRICIA. No it's not SOS, Sean.

SEAN. You see I need to get inside.

He starts to bang on the glass.

PATRICIA. It's all right. We just need to move your walker.

SEAN. But then I can't stand?

PATRICIA. You can stand, Sean.

SEAN. No!

No. No. I'm falling.

PATRICIA. You're not falling.

He smashes the glass with his fist… it shatters.

She screams.

Jesus!

SEAN (*in exactly the same tone and turning now in circles, totally distressed with his hand bleeding heavily*). Jesus!

PATRICIA. I'm sorry.

SEAN. Jesus!

PATRICIA. I'm sorry, Sean.

SEAN. SOS!

It's SOS!

PATRICIA. Please… you need to calm down.

SEAN. I need to be inside!

He hits the glass again – it shatters! An alarm rages.

End of scene.

Scene Five

The stage is set as in the opening scene, though there is cardboard over the broken windowpane. There is a handbag and cake box and car keys on the table. SEAN is alone. He is back in his wheelchair. PATRICIA enters upstage, she is wearing a headscarf and sunglasses. She closes the door and stands with her back to the wall. SEAN doesn't move.

PATRICIA. Psssst!

No response.

Sean!

SEAN *goes to rise.*

It's okay – don't stir yourself!

He looks at her. She lifts her glasses.

It's me! Patricia.

No response.

How are you?

SEAN. I... I am... (*Trails away.*)

PATRICIA. God!

And how is your poor hand?

SEAN. My... my hand is mending thank you.

PATRICIA. Sean!

No response.

Sean! I am so sorry. I am just so sorry about everything...

No response.

They wouldn't let me in!

No response.

I'm barred! Can you believe that?

They say you're a flight risk! But I just stationed myself outside that door, I wouldn't budge and then I thought Sunday! If I can wait till Sunday then Dee will come and they will waddle off and I'll get in. And it worked, the plan worked, because here I am!

Here I am, Sean.

No response.

Oh God!

Can't you hear me?

SEAN. I can.

I can hear you.

PATRICIA. Thank you, Jesus!

But can you forgive me?

SEAN. Forgive you?

PATRICIA. Yes please.

SEAN. But of course.

PATRICIA. Because I know I upset you.

SEAN. No no.

PATRICIA. I did. I know I did.

And when I couldn't come in.

And I couldn't see you.

Well! I didn't want you to think.

I didn't want you to think I'd just gone.

SEAN. Oh!

Thank you.

PATRICIA. Because I would never do that.

I could never do that, Sean.

Because I'm fond. I'm so terribly fond of you.

SEAN. Ahh!

PATRICIA. And all those things… those terrible things I said about you and Tom…

SEAN (*alarmed*). No!

PATRICIA. I'm sorry – that's all. That's all I wanted to say because you're right… you are perfectly right. I don't know him. I don't know Tom and I don't know anything, Sean, because I'm just… I'm just so lost here. I'm lost. And that's my problem… because I was never lost at home.

SEAN. I see.

PATRICIA. Yes.

Pause.

Thank God you're all right.

SEAN. I'm fine. Just fine.

PATRICIA. Because I was worried. I was really worried, Sean.

I thought I'd done real damage.

Driven you out of your mind!

SEAN. I've been out of my mind for years.

She laughs.

PATRICIA. Well!

SEAN. No harm done!

PATRICIA. That's good.

Short pause.

And have they been minding you well?

SEAN. Eh…

PATRICIA. Has that matron changed your bandage because there's always the chance of infection…

SEAN. She has.

PATRICIA. Oh! That's good.

Good, Sean.

SEAN. Yes.

She comes over and gently examines it.

PATRICIA. Still, it looks quite nasty!

SEAN. It's nothing.

PATRICIA. Maybe!… For the hardy buck!

SEAN. Yes.

Pause.

And how have you been?

PATRICIA. Me?

SEAN. Yes.

PATRICIA. Distracted!

SEAN. Ah!

PATRICIA. What with the worry of you!

SEAN. I'm so sorry…

PATRICIA. And still no sign of Nora. And the matron-bitch on the warpath. I'll tell you, I scarcely felt I'd see the end of the week!

SEAN. Oh dear.

Are you not well?

PATRICIA. Not well?

Not well, Sean? Jesus!

Slight pause.

It's just…

SEAN. What?

PATRICIA. Well…

I think I know I am going to die.

SEAN. Die?

PATRICIA. Yes.

From the next stroke or the next.

SEAN. But…

PATRICIA. I took a turn, you see…

SEAN. A turn?

PATRICIA. Yes. Thursday… only Thursday…

It was a class of a fit! Now not the full monty, but enough to cause a blackout, a fall.

SEAN. My goodness…

PATRICIA. Yes.

So I don't believe, you see. I mean, I no longer believe that there's a tablet, Sean... a different tablet that might stop all this.

There is a silence.

SEAN. I see.

PATRICIA. Yes.

Pause.

And do you know it's hard to go.

SEAN. Is it?

PATRICIA. Yes. For some of us.

But at least I'm not afraid.

SEAN. Aren't you?

PATRICIA. No.

And that's the curious thing because I was afraid before. I was anxious, so terribly anxious of the darkness... and the heat... and being alone. Sure that's why I came in here. Why I eventually agreed.

Now I just hope it comes up quick so we don't have to sell.

SEAN. Dear God...

PATRICIA. I was doing the calculations.

And I know I can't last long.

I won't leave Nora stranded, Sean.

SEAN. No.

PATRICIA. Not when there's no hope. No hope for me.

But my prognosis is suitably drastic so that's the upside.

SEAN. Is it?

PATRICIA. Yes. Now that they've started... again.

The fits.

SEAN. I see.

Slight pause.

PATRICIA. But I just wish I could see Nora, Sean! Calm her!
  She feels so bloody far away!

SEAN. Then why don't you go home?

PATRICIA. Go home?

SEAN. Wouldn't that solve everything?

PATRICIA. Go home?

SEAN. Yes.

PATRICIA. But how?

SEAN. In the car of course.

  Dee's car!

PATRICIA. Dee's car?

SEAN. It's right outside.

PATRICIA. I know it is but...

SEAN. Wasn't that always the plan?

PATRICIA. No!

  Well, not really. Just a thought. A while back. A scheme.
  There's not a chance that we could do it... it's just a hare-
  brained scheme.

SEAN. Why so?

PATRICIA. Because... because how? We couldn't... I
  couldn't... I mean, we couldn't just go...?

SEAN. Why not?

PATRICIA. Because... there's Matron... and doctors.... and all
  my stuff!

SEAN. What stuff?

PATRICIA. Medication!

SEAN. Which you just said was useless!

PATRICIA. Yes I did, didn't I.

SEAN. Don't stay if you're not afraid, Patricia.

She pauses.

PATRICIA. I am not afraid.

Pause.

And you'll come too?

SEAN. No.

PATRICIA. You will.

SEAN. No.

PATRICIA. But I won't go without you!

SEAN. You'll have to.

PATRICIA. No.

Please, Sean…

SEAN. I can't.

PATRICIA. Of course you can!

SEAN. No. I'm sorry, Patricia.

I don't… I just don't have the strength to face it again.

PATRICIA. But you're dead in here!

SEAN. I'm safe in here.

PATRICIA. Because I've seen you, Sean. I've known you. And it's all still in there, isn't it. You're still in there! Your theatre. Your life!

SEAN. Well then, I have everything I need.

Slight pause.

PATRICIA. Not even for Tom?

No response.

I'll take you to Tom!

SEAN. No.

No, Patricia.

Tom has someone else.

Slight pause.

PATRICIA. Christ.

Well, isn't he the fool.

Slight pause.

He's the fool, Sean.

SEAN. You should go back to your life, Patricia.

Go back while you can.

It's a gift to want to go home.

Pause.

PATRICIA *deliberates.*

PATRICIA. Just to see it. To see my garden! And my cushions and my cat! It's ridiculous!

SEAN. It's not.

PATRICIA. I feel I am no one out here.

SEAN. I know.

PATRICIA. Just no one.

SEAN. Except to me.

Pause.

PATRICIA. Sean…

SEAN. Please.

You have no idea how h-happy I'll be, how happy. If I can do this, this one thing. For you.

Now take those keys.

PATRICIA. Take the keys?

SEAN. Yes

PATRICIA. Oh God!

Yes.

Okay!

SEAN. Good girl.

I knew you would.

She picks up the keys.

PATRICIA. Do you know I've never stolen anything in my life.

SEAN. I'm sure I can explain.

PATRICIA. But I'm going to miss you.

SEAN. I'm going to miss you too.

PATRICIA. So come with me. I'll mind you. Me and Nora.

We won't care if you put the cups in the fridge.

Pause. He looks at her.

Pause.

So what…?

SEAN. What?

PATRICIA. I just walk out that door?

SEAN. It would seem so!

PATRICIA. And walk to the car?

SEAN. Exactly.

PATRICIA. Okay!

SEAN. Okay?

PATRICIA. I'm off!

SEAN. Good woman!

PATRICIA. I'll say goodbye so.

SEAN. Do.

PATRICIA. Goodbye, Sean.

SEAN. Goodbye.

She stands. She not quite sure how to part. So she blows him a kiss.

He smiles.

PATRICIA. You won't forget me?

SEAN. I can't promise anything!

She smiles. He smiles. She turns and walks to the door.

She grabs a hold of the handle but stalls.

PATRICIA. Goodness.

SEAN. Is everything all right?

PATRICIA. Em. Yes it is. It is.

It's just…

SEAN. What?

PATRICIA. I think I feel quite hot.

SEAN. Do you?

PATRICIA. Of a sudden…

She stalls.

SEAN. Perhaps it's just the excitement?

PATRICIA. No.

I don't think so.

It feels a little hard to breathe.

SEAN. Patricia!

PATRICIA (*quietly*). Sean…

SEAN. I'll pull the cord.

PATRICIA. No don't!

Please don't.

SEAN. But I must!

PATRICIA. No.

No, Sean.

Don't I know now I'll be fine.

Blackout.

End of scene.

Scene Six

SEAN *sits alone in the conservatory. The cardboard is still in place. His arm is still bandaged. The door upstage opens. SEAN goes to rise but no one enters. He sits. He now takes a black tie from his pocket. He starts to try to put it on. He struggles to tie it. He finds he cannot get the knot. He leaves it hanging around his neck. He sits.*

He eyes the walker. It is almost out of reach but with his foot he manages to gently guide it to him. He attempts to stand, once, twice. He is up on his feet. He smiles. He moves about on the walker. He stops. He looks over to the CD player. He inches over. He fiddles with the CD player. The music comes on very, very loud. He panics and pulls at it and it falls to the ground. The music stops. He is relieved.

He stands now motionless on his walker. He closes his eyes. He starts to finger the notes in the air as he had done in the earlier scene as he remembers the music in his mind. He smiles. He puts his hand to the window, to the outside world and he whispers 'Goodbye'.

The light closes in around him like a spotlight, until all is black.

The End.

A Nick Hern Book

HALCYON DAYS first published in Great Britain in 2012 as a paperback
original by Nick Hern Books Limited, The Glasshouse, 49a Goldhawk Road,
London W12 8QP, in association with Tall Tales Theatre Company

Cover photograph by Pat Redmond with Anita Reeves as Patricia and Stephen
Brennan as Sean
Cover design by Ned Hoste, 2H

Typeset by Nick Hern Books, London
Printed in Great Britain by Mimeo Ltd, Huntingdon, Cambridgeshire PE29 6XX

A CIP catalogue record for this book is available from the British Library

ISBN 978 1 84842 301 5

Woodland
CARBON
www.woodlandcarbon.co.uk
NICK HERN BOOKS
Printed on Carbon Captured paper